I0499215

THIS NOTEBOOK

BELONGS TO

NOTEBOOK

NOTEBOOK

NOTEBOOK

NOTEBOOK

NOTEBOOK

NOTEBOOK

NOTEBOOK

NOTEBOOK

NOTEBOOK

NOTEBOOK

NOTEBOOK

NOTEBOOK

NOTEBOOK

NOTEBOOK

NOTEBOOK

NOTEBOOK

NOTEBOOK

NOTEBOOK

NOTEBOOK

NOTEBOOK

NOTEBOOK

NOTEBOOK

NOTEBOOK

NOTEBOOK

NOTEBOOK

NOTEBOOK

NOTEBOOK

NOTEBOOK

NOTEBOOK

NOTEBOOK

NOTEBOOK

NOTEBOOK

NOTEBOOK

NOTEBOOK

NOTEBOOK

NOTEBOOK

NOTEBOOK

NOTEBOOK

NOTEBOOK

NOTEBOOK

NOTEBOOK

NOTEBOOK

NOTEBOOK

NOTEBOOK

NOTEBOOK

NOTEBOOK

NOTEBOOK

NOTEBOOK

NOTEBOOK

NOTEBOOK

NOTEBOOK

NOTEBOOK

NOTEBOOK

NOTEBOOK

NOTEBOOK

NOTEBOOK

NOTEBOOK

NOTEBOOK

NOTEBOOK

NOTEBOOK

NOTEBOOK

www.ingramcontent.com/pod-product-compliance
Lightning Source LLC
Chambersburg PA
CBHW070429220526
45466CB00004B/1602
* 9 7 8 1 6 7 7 7 9 4 2 7 0 *